SOVEREIGN FRAMEWORK

The antidote for America's pandemic of narcissism

DICK ERVASTI

Ervasti & Company Worldwide

570 West 78th Street #2001
Chanhassen, MN 55317-2001

©2010 Ervasti & Company Worldwide, Chanhassen, MN USA

All rights reserved, including the rights to reproduce this book or portions thereof in any form whatsoever. For information contact Ervasti & Company Worldwide, Subsidiary Rights Inquiry, 570 West 78th Street, Chanhassen, MN 55317-2001 USA

The global E device is a trademark of Ervasti & Company Worldwide.

For information on special discounts for bulk purchases, please contact Ervasti & Co. Bulk Procurement at 1 866 401-4633, or email admin@ervasti.com

First Digital Printing: September 2010

ISBN - 13: 978-1-4505-8907-9
ISBN - 10:   1-4505-8907-3

*To Mary, my dear wife,
and partner for life.*

Sovereign Framework

Table of Contents

Look in the Mirror 1
The Rolling Stop 9
"You Deserve It!" 15
Passing the Baton 23
Academic Alchemy 31
Heads or Tails 43
Just who IS the enemy? 57
Settling the Score 73

Introduction

Look in the Mirror

If you think I am being rhetorical, you are wrong. Get up and look at yourself in the mirror while I ask you a few questions. Ideally, I'd like you to ask yourself these questions *out loud*. As you answer them, I want you to notice the expression on your face.

Do you love yourself? How much do you love yourself? More than anyone else? Less than anyone else? Less than you should? Are you making all the money you'd like to make in this lifetime? Do you have control over your life? Do you like to control others? Why? How often do you do what the *cool crowd* does instead of doing what you *know* is right?

Sovereign Framework

How many people did you hurt today? Why? How many people did you help today? How many people did you smile at, having no agenda, hidden or otherwise? Are you amazing? Why? Or, if not, why not? Are you good at something? Smart? Good looking? Witty? Rich? Who cares? Why?

When you come to a stop sign, are you a roller or a full-stopper? Do you have a lead foot? Like to speed? Maybe even a little? Everyone does it, right? Are you above the law? It's okay to break the law; it's just not okay to get caught, right?

Whatever that thing is that you are good at, do you somehow use it for emotional or psychological leverage in your relationships? How quickly do you pre-judge people as being either above you, equal to you, or beneath you? Do you *kiss up* to those above? Do you deride and belittle those beneath? Why? If not, why not?

Speaking of hurt, who has hurt you? Do you want to get back at them? Why? Will it make you feel better? Why do you need to feel better? When was the last time you

Look in the Mirror

felt pain? Rejection pain? Financial pain? Moral pain? When was the last time you committed a sin? Why? Who cares?

How often do you find it necessary to cover your ass? Why do you think you need to cover your ass? Are you a blamer or an owner-upper? Are you perfect? Why? Who would you most like to be? Why? Who cares? Why? Are you hot? Are you powerful? Are you rich? How does it feel to be like that? How would you feel if you weren't that way?

Are you a *tech gadget* freak? Why? Do those things make you feel a certain way? Why? What would your life be like if you didn't have gadgets? Why? Do you know who you are without any gadgets? Do you know who you are without your friends? What if someone took away all your personal power things and all your friends for one year? How would you feel about that? Why?

One final question: when was the last time you had such a quick and intense self-examination session exactly like this? It's hard work. Also, it is quite likely that at least some of the questions brought up some sensitive issues. If so, good. That means I have prepared you with the proper mindset for reading *Sovereign Framework*.

This booklet is strictly my opinion. I try to provide factual information and include any sources along the way, but the data I offer is not scientific by any means. However, as scientists on both sides of the *Darwinism/design* debate will tell you, sometimes you go with what you have, even though it is not at all statistically robust, because not going with anything is no decision at all.

It should come as no surprise that, being a member of the media, I tend to be a content junkie. I monitor various arcane facets of society. I ask a lot of questions along the way (ya think?!). Sometimes, answers are nowhere to be found. Often, however, I find one or two. Once in a while, I find that I have collected enough answers to form a conclusion, or at least a theory, about various matters.

I began one such monitoring study on a warm and sunny day in May 1997. My limousine was taking me through the beautiful upscale streets of Santa Monica, California.

Look in the Mirror

On this particular day, my driver, Gilles, had chosen to take a route that passed by the junior high school, just as it was letting out. My mind was wandering to and fro, thinking about my next voiceover session, or where my wife Mary & I should have dinner that evening. Suddenly, my attention was captured by a very lovely and sexy female who was walking provocatively down the street alongside the limo. She wore a tight-fitting top, low-riding jeans, and *smooch-me* heels. The view was startling. "If only I was single," I chuckled to myself. And then I realized I was looking at one of the *ninth-grade students* who were just getting out of school for the day. In an instant, my thoughts turned from casual to horrific. Then, I began to look at the other kids as they walked down the street. That day I calculated at least twenty-five percent of those young girls were dressed very nearly like the hookers I'd just seen about fifteen minutes earlier on Sunset Boulevard! Why? How?

After living nearly seven years in Los Angeles, we moved in 1999 back to our hometown of the Twin Cities in Minnesota. I experienced nothing short of culture shock. Just as much culture shock, in fact, as I felt when this naive Minnesotan first set foot on California soil in 1993. I wasn't quite prepared to deal with the stark urban realities of homelessness, gang culture, wandering moral compasses, and depressing air quality. I thought, "How good it would be to get back home!" But, much to my chagrin, the pervasive and inexorable wave of entitlement and apathy among young people in Minnesota almost precisely matched that of California.

Irish statesman, Edmund Burke, once said, "All that is necessary for the triumph of evil is that good men do nothing." If that statement has meaning for you, I am sad to say that we good people of America have collectively done *nothing for far too long.* Why are we seeing the general decline of morals and values in our society? We, the vast, easy-going, good-natured, relatively peace-keeping, God-fearing, and above all *free* people, have lazily sat around (since even long before the *American Revolution*) and witnessed the atrophy of very nearly ALL that is dear to us as a free people.

How did that happen? Why? I do not blame anyone but myself. I posit that you, dear reader, should also hold yourself equally accountable. We shall have no blame-game here.

When this work originally appeared on my blog, it was entitled *Pandemic of Narcissism*. But, being a praying man, I found the Holy Spirit prompting me to title the booklet for the solution it offers rather than the problem it examines.

So, let us get ready, you and I, to *take full responsibility* for the future of America.

Let the journey begin!

Sovereign Framework

Chapter 1

The Rolling Stop

I can't even begin to count how many times the topic of the general decline of American society has popped up in conversation with family and friends over the years. Clearly, it's on everyone's mind, but it seems when the discussion steers toward identifying possible causes, the momentum slows and comes to a halt without the presentation of any compelling conclusions.

As is often the case with such an immense challenge, I decided to isolate an example in everyday life from which I could draw on a fairly large body of empirical evidence: the enormous decline in the percentage of motorists who *actually come to a complete stop* at stop signs. Instead they employ the so-called "rolling stop." This seemingly harmless habit proved to be an excellent starting point because you can often learn more about a society by observing its subconscious actions; driving is an excellent example of this.

Over the past ten years, I've probably observed about 25,000 instances of people's driving habits as they approach a stop sign. At the beginning of my observations, roughly 40% of drivers came to a complete and total stop. By 2009, however, that metric was down to less than 15%.

At the onset of my empirical work, another very personal metric came to my attention: I had not been stopping at stops signs either. When seeking to find the causes of this, I concluded that I felt like I was so busy, I really couldn't take the time to come to a complete stop. I thought that I was somehow special, and thus arrived at the de facto conclusion that I was above the law. Wow. I immediately changed my habits and now I always come to a complete stop at stop signs. I also drive the speed limit.

The Rolling Stop

Most states have a law against rolling stops that generally reads as follows,

"A complete stop is when there is no forward momentum and the needle on the speedometer is at 0. In a rolling stop, the car wheels are still in motion and the car is moving at less than 5 mph. Failing to come to a complete stop at a stop sign is a traffic violation."

Although the specific wording varies by state, the rolling stop is a traffic violation in all 50 states in America. Also, the longer the stop, the more discernable it is to the naked eye, and the less chance there is that the motorist would receive a ticket.

Along the way, I discovered that the term *rolling stop* had another nickname: "The California Stop." Suddenly, numerous light bulbs started shining brightly for me! My wife Mary and I had a chance to live in California on two occasions totaling eight years between 1993 and 2004. I can tell you without doubt that hardly anyone living in California has stopped at a stop sign for a very long time.

I concluded that the cause of this problem was what I call the *culture of narcissism*[1] so prevalent in California.

Dictionary.com, which sites numerous sources, defines **narcissism** as:

"**An inordinate fascination with oneself; excessive self-love; vanity.**"

A second entry defines it as:

"**A psychological condition characterized by self-preoccupation, lack of empathy, and unconscious deficits in self-esteem.**"

The last phrase is arguably the most important characteristic of all in searching for the causes of narcissism: unconscious deficits in self-esteem. As we dig deeper, and by necessity get a little geeky, we will certainly find that the deficit usually occurs when the person has experienced an inadequate amount of external emotional sup-

---

[1] I wrote this chapter in January 2010. To show you how I just don't get out much, it turns out that **Christopher Lasch** wrote an excellent book of the very same title in 1979. Doh!

port during the first few years of their life. This does not always lead to narcissism, but there exists what I am going to label *a toggle threshold* whereby, depending on other factors (*i.e.,* genetic, environmental, etc.), the person is either taken down a path of conscious inadequacy or unconscious. In the case of the unconscious path, one of those factors tends be an outstanding characteristic or trait the person inevitably uses to mask the deficit. It typically comes in the form of good looks, musical or athletic talent, intelligence, or a clever wit.

Whatever the person's outstanding trait may be, they usually resort to devoting all their life-energy to it. The result is a general attitude that makes them feel and act quite special and extraordinary. When this occurs, they are said to have created a *narcissistic anchor*. Unless the person is introduced to another more healthy and overwhelming influence, they will remain in a *narcissistic loop* indefinitely.

So, why am I targeting California as being so nearly collectively narcissistic? People there who are at risk of the deficit, and there are millions, have a vast array of social and environmental anchors they can invest in or become attached to: beautiful weather, show business, and demographic diversity, to name a few. This is in addition to any individual anchors that are most certainly available to many. Thus, it is much easier to see the multiple layers of causes that have created the culture of narcissism in the state.

But are cultural conditions extreme enough to justify the label *pandemic?* Pathological narcissism is occurring everywhere in America, and there presently seems to be no end in sight to its prolific growth.

Chapter 2

"You Deserve It!"

In order for a pandemic to develop, there are two prerequisites: a point of entry, and no viable means of defense against it. In *Chapter One,* we examined the culture of narcissism in the state of California. While its sociological dynamics make it a great example, both historical and present-day, of a point of entry for the seeds of narcissism, we will soon see how *all urban areas,* and by extension, all of America, have allowed this damaging disease to take root.

It was September 1945, and American soldiers were coming home from WWII to exuberant crowds. Simply put, it was a great time to be an American. The Allied Forces had just defeated the enemies of the free world and the entire nation was experiencing an overwhelming sense of *victory* and *empowerment*. As soldiers resumed their civilian lives, that feeling of empowerment was transferred to all spheres of American culture. Thus, the seeds of narcissism were able to find yet another[2] point of entry. Unsuspecting Americans, preoccupied with living a good and honest life in the wake of a valid and hard-fought victory, were oblivious to this tiny invasion.

For several years, the economy boomed, with waves upon waves of entrepreneurship and innovation leading the way. Nowhere was this more evident than in the American advertising industry.

By 1960, many advertising agencies were starting to use a certain form of qualitative research known as *focus groups*. The technique originated at the Bureau of Applied Social Research at Columbia University. The idea of a focus group is to formally gather a group of consumers and ask them their opinions about a product, service,

---

[2] As we will examine in *Chapter Three,* the actual first point of entry happened during the narcissistic excesses of the Roaring Twenties.

"You Deserve it!"

concept, advertisement, idea, or even packaging. These responses would be collected into sets of data which would later be analyzed using statistical and other scientific methods. Companies would then take the data and use it to market their brands to the public.

Some companies would also use the data to create new inventions. This was easily possible because, by now, that sense of empowerment felt by individuals years before was now fully embedded in American society. The "I can do anything!" attitude began showing up in focus group data in various forms. Businesses responded with new and exciting products that helped support this attitude, and consumers took to these new offerings very quickly. You needn't look far at all to see evidence of this. Just step into your kitchen to see the likes of automatic can-openers, microwave ovens, coffeemakers with timers, prepackaged heat 'n' serve dinners; the list is endless. Even in recessionary times, advertisers would just turn up the heat on their messages. If a luxury item seemed a bit too costly, they would simply add three soothing words onto the ad's call-to-action: *"You deserve it!"*

Despite all this engineered euphoria, however, narcissism often had a difficult time taking root, for a majority of Americans still possessed high degrees of personal character, integrity, honesty, psychological boundaries, a good work ethic, and concern for the common good.

Even so, narcissism found powerful allies in the advertising industry and the print and electronic media (henceforth, collectively, *the media*). By the mid-1980's, radio and TV had fully adopted the same qualitative research techniques used by the ad agencies. They conducted focus groups on everything from news, weather, and sports, to music and talk-show content. Somewhere along the way, journalistic integrity was sacrificed[3] on the altar of market research. The media, thus relieved of the burden of telling Americans the truth, carried on with the much simpler task of telling Americans what they wanted to hear.

Meanwhile, in the home, families began facing new and alarming challenges. By the 1970's, the **empowerment**

---
[3] For expansion, visit **http://ervasti.com/broadcast**

paradigm was charging an ever steeper price for its privileges. As the media promoted an endless parade of products and services, many families discovered they were spending beyond their means to sustain the feeling. In the face of these extra demands, a growing number of households saw the need for both parents to work full-time, a solution which happily coincided with the media's cry for equality in the workplace and women's liberation. Suddenly, narcissism found rich new soil that enabled it to grow a deep, strong and powerful root system.

Children need a strong foundation of authority, trust and emotional connection in their parental relationships. It helps them build their own ***sovereign framework*** of personal character, integrity, honesty, psychological boundaries, a good work ethic, and concern for the common good. By the mid-1980's, with both parents working full-time in a majority of homes, there began a steep decline, both quantitatively and qualitatively, in relationships between parents and children.

So, let's do the math. Less parental availability leads to

less connectedness, which in turn, for the children, leads to a lack of skills for developing the framework.

Parents tried their best, but because they were quite preoccupied placating the demands of the empowerment paradigm, all they could convey to their children was the *top-of-mind* notion that "You can do anything you want!" This idea is harmless and even encouraging when the sovereign framework exists to moderate it and govern its meaning, but it is a recipe for confusion, depression, anxiety, despair, and low self-esteem absent the framework. As we learned in *Chapter One,* an important aspect of narcissism is a profound and unconscious deficit in self-esteem. It should come as no surprise, then, that in a matter of just a few years in the 1980's, narcissism began bearing ripe, juicy fruit, and dropping its seeds everywhere.

The disconnect between parents and children often became exacerbated when "empowered" spouses, embroiled in conflicts of commitment to both marriage and self, chose divorce as the solution to their problems. The implicit message to the children: "We love you, but the emotional support structure you need from us is now offline and unavailable."

Many guilt-ridden parents, divorced or otherwise, also tried to supplement the ironically labeled "quality time" by taking a materialistic approach, gifting their children with the latest clothing fashions for school, electronic games, music devices, computers, generous allowance money, and even new cars when they were able to obtain a drivers license. Some of these bribes were procured on credit, which created the illusion of wealth and added yet another narcissistic anchor to the already attractive array of choices. Thus, the ***golden era of entitlement*** was born.

We have now established multiple points of entry, and also demonstrated how the overall decline in the emotional health of the American family severely weakened our defenses against the attack of narcissism. But, even with all this relentless growth, the situation has not yet reached the point of a pandemic in our story. The children must grow up a bit and become fully functioning members of the empowerment paradigm. In *Chapter Three,* we step back a bit further in time and look at a larger window of the 20th century. As we examine each new American generation, we discover the development of a perfect storm that today threatens the very foundations of America.

Chapter 3

Passing the Baton

Because we are comparing narcissism to a virus, there must exist an incubation period during which the person being attacked is unaware of the invasion. As we continue our examination using this viral correlation, we will learn that real viruses and other pathogens can only wish for the *stealthy* incubation characteristics of narcissism.

Narcissism is unique in that, after an incubation period of indeterminate duration, it never actually trumpets its arrival in a host. Also, its initial symptoms vary quite dramatically from person to person, making it nearly impossible for any individual or society to ascertain that an attack is under way and defensive action must be taken.

This is especially true if the host is lacking a fully developed sovereign framework (which we learned about in *Chapter Two*).

To understand this pattern of stealth on a sociological scale, we must look back in time to before the *Great Depression.* In the wake of WWI, America had been experiencing the debaucherous decade of modernity known as the Roaring Twenties. Although a majority of Americans each possessed the core values that make for a strong sovereign framework, there was still the temptation to dabble in excessive consumption of such things as fashion, moving pictures, radio, and the arts. It is here where the seeds that grow and become our present-day pandemic find their first point of entry into American culture. While Americans were living it up, narcissism found a nice little spot to incubate.

During the 1920's, the American economy was booming. But, later in the decade, it acquired a fever in the form of an asset bubble in common stocks. To add fuel to the fire, the U.S. Federal Reserve Bank, in the late 1920's, began to systematically shrink the nation's money supply in an attempt to limit the risks of inflation. On Tuesday October 29, 1929, also known as *Black Tuesday,* investors began to act on the realization that the wild upward climb of the market could not possibly last forever. The wave of selling resulted in a crash of the U.S. equities market and a steep decline in both U.S. exports and U.S. GNP (referred to in present-day as GDP).

Over the ensuing months and years during the Great Depression, the Dow Jones Industrial Average lost 89 percent of its value. By 1933, U.S. unemployment skyrocketed to 25 percent. Many people experienced the triple shock of unemployment, total loss of savings and investments, and the loss of large assets such as homes and automobiles. Thus, the term depression came to mean much more than the mere macroeconomic reference.

The people who lived through the Great Depression were of three distinct generations: chronologically, the *Lost Generation* (born in the 1880's), the *Greatest Generation* (born between 1918-1925), and the *Silent Generation* (born between 1925-1945). Only the Lost Generation had experienced a previous economic downturn: the *Long*

Depression from 1873-1896. They arguably weathered the storm better than the other two generations. However, by the end of the Great Depression, the majority of Americans had lost their ambition and zest for life.

The youngest generation, the Silents, were particularly disconnected and fatalistic, possessing little or no ability to develop their own sovereign framework because their parents, the Losts, were preoccupied dealing with the economic crisis. Even if the Silents could somehow have discovered the attack of narcissism they and their parents sustained during the Roaring Twenties, they had no viable means of defense against it. Therefore, all throughout the Great Depression, narcissism was able to quietly continue incubating itself in the psyche of Americans, most notably the Silent Generation.

If human history demonstrates anything, it certainly could be the tendency for a culture to swing from one extreme to the other, coming to rest in the middle only rarely if ever. Such could easily be said of America's transition from the economic instability of the Great Depression to the near sudden and profound economic growth brought on by WWII.

On a sociological level, Americans in general, and the Silent Generation in particular, somehow needed to sweep away the negative memories of the depression and prove to themselves that life was, indeed, worth living. But, there is a great risk in this notion. The Silents, in the main, lacked a sovereign framework, which by definition, helps to sustain the individual's internal resolve to observe and conduct life in moderation, while also protecting the individual from extreme, grandiose choices and dangerous threats both internal and external. So, on a subconscious level, they were betting on the external factor of a WWII victory to help them turn their luck around. In other words, they were doing the sociological equivalent of *gambling* with the highest stakes of all: their injured, conflicted and hopeless world-view. By doing so, they unwittingly set in motion the optimal conditions for not only another point of entry for more seeds of narcissism, but also a pathway by which those seeds already in incubation could spread and eventually flourish.

Sovereign Framework

We have now recognized what "the Baton" is as well as those in our story who presently carry it: members of the Greatest Generation and the Silent Generation (henceforth, *Boomer Parents*), who of course give birth to the *Baby Boomer Generation* and the early cohorts of *Generation X*.

In *Chapter Two*, we examined American culture in the wake of the Allied Forces' Victory in WWII. In light of the above gambling observation, it is easy to see why many Boomer Parents had no difficulty using the war victory as a proxy for the outcome of their risky wager. The **empowerment paradigm** was thus born. They saw themselves as coming home the clear winners; a perception that by itself would easily become a narcissistic anchor. All it takes is one anchor for narcissism to spread like wildfire in a person and cause the formation of a *narcissistic world-view*. So, as Baby Boomers grew into adulthood, they simply adapted their Boomer Parents' world-view to their own sub-culture, added a few more anchors such as rock 'n' roll, drug experimentation, and with the media's help, independence from the status-quo, and "the Baton" had now been successfully passed on to them, causing narcissism to spread out its roots and entrench itself deeper into the American psyche.

In *Chapter Four,* the Baby Boomers and their younger siblings, Generation X, grow up, have *Generation Y* (or *millennial*) kids, and send them off to college to sit under the instruction and leadership of other Baby Boomer and Gen X professors. For you see, by this time, educators have no problem using the classroom and the lab as social engineering tools to sustain and proliferate narcissism, which in our story, has now grown into an epidemic in American culture.

Sovereign Framework

Chapter 4

Academic Alchemy

One of narcissism's unique symptoms is the *fundamental duality* characterized by an inflated sense of self-worth along with a heightened denial of the deficit in self-esteem.

Left unchecked, the disease often leads the person down a false life-path typified by delusion, frustration, lack of co-operation from others, failure, and angst (frequently mistaken for intense passion, usually in the context of one or more narcissistic anchors). When this life-path has played itself out over a period of years, there tends to be repeated cycles of alternating extreme outcomes; euphoric false-hope followed by a crash-and-burn scenario (the *narcissistic-loop* we examined in *Chapter One*). The amplitude of each of these cycles remains fairly constant unless the person discovers and adopts additional narcissistic anchors, or of course, until they encounter and are influenced by a *higher standard* that helps them build a strong sovereign framework.

One very powerful social phenomenon many adopt is the *community anchor:* a group, formal or informal, of like-minded narcissists, many or all of whom share common interest in one or more personal anchors. A group can be comprised of just two, or millions. Examples are: a high school clique, a band of musicians, the fans of a band, actor, or show, buyers of a product, users of a specific mechanical apparatus (*i.e.,* car, motorcycle, mobile phone, video game, music device, file-sharing, social-networking, etc.), and even adherents to a theory, philosophy or opinion. Community anchors tend to exacerbate each participant's fundamental duality and cause them to drift further away from opportunities to identify and decelerate their damaging behavior patterns.

Although there are countless examples of narcissistic communities in America, one of the more dangerous has roots extending back to the 19th century: the sphere of *education*. There have been, and certainly are important exceptions in education, but in the main, narcissists in academia have built a robust community with a rich history of attempts to control the developmental path of society. Their primary mission was, and still is in present-day, to form and sustain a collective response to the wild socio-economic swings and residual challenges inherent in the Industrial Revolution; in essence, narcissists creating a huge anchor out of the task of attempting to control certain other narcissistic tendencies in culture.

Much of the initial fuel and inspiration for this community's activities can be found in the philosophies of **Karl Marx.** Of particular interest was Marx's *theory of alienation,* which posits that, especially in a capitalist society, the individual becomes separated from their purpose or destiny because they lose control over their actions and are thus never able to become self-fulfilled. Marx did not limit this theory to social structures; he also extended it into religion, concluding that the notion of a God usurps man's inherent ability to conceive spontaneous and independent thought and to derive a sense of fulfillment from taking action on that thought.

My empirical research of narcissistic communities indicates a high probability that Marx and his mentor, benefactor, and colleague, **Friedrich Engels,** created their own community and anchored themselves to it sometime around 1844. Both Marx and Engels suffered from a deficit in self-esteem. Biographical works about the two indicate that Engels did not receive enough familial nurturing to develop his sovereign framework; his father was a dedicated capitalist. Marx received some nurturing from his father, a lawyer who was steeped in the so-called *enlightenment movement.* However, Marx also failed to develop his own framework, and instead, sought medication for his pain in the new German philosophy of *Left Hegelianism,* which led him to view all paths to faith, and to capitalism, as antagonistic.

Narcissism requires anchors to redirect the person's thought away from their self-esteem deficit and toward a dream-like, utopian, and grandiose world-view, often casting the person (or persons, in the context of a community) in a top leadership or founder's role. So, two intelligent yet subconsciously miserable people, Marx and Engels, found solace and support in each other's company and ideas. Hence, the initial structure was created for attacking capitalism and religion via *Marxism* and its later iterations such as *progressivism, socialism,* and *postmodernism.*

Even so, Marxist infiltration of education did not catch on in America until 1901, when a college socialist club was organized at the University of Wisconsin in Madison. Later, in December 1904, a group of elitist socialist intellectuals including authors **Upton Sinclair** and **Jack London,** publicist **Leonard Abbott,** lawyer **Clarence Darrow,** activist **Florence Kelley,** and industrialist socialite **Graham Phelps Stokes** (husband of activist **Rose Pastor Stokes**) signed a document drafted by Sinclair calling for the establishment of the *Intercollegiate Socialist Society (ISS)* to, as was put forth in the document,

"... promote an intelligent interest in socialism among college men and women."

It is also important to note the family backgrounds of nearly every one of the signatories to this agreement:

· *Upton Sinclair's* father was an alcoholic and therefore unable to help nurture a young Upton to help build his sovereign framework.

· *Jack London* was born out of wedlock. The father sought to have the baby aborted. The mother, instead, shot herself in the final months of pregnancy. The wound was not serious, but she was mentally deranged, so both of London's parents were emotionally unavailable to support the development of his framework.

· *Clarence Darrow's* mother, **Emily Eddy Darrow**, was an early advocate of women's rights; whatever framework she helped young Clarence build was arguably tainted with progressive thought.

- *Florence Kelley's* father, **William Darrah Kelley,** worked for numerous political and social reforms. Kelley herself engaged Engels in frequent correspondence.

- *Graham Phelps Stokes* and his wife, Rose, both came from progressive families. Rose Pastor Stokes' parents separated and abandoned her when she was three years old, leaving her with no framework, but a beautiful talent for writing, which she easily used as a narcissistic anchor, as became evident in her activist articles.

All these people were children during the Long Depression from 1873-1896.

With its formation, the ISS became the first organized and active branch of *American Marxism,* and its status as a narcissistic community anchor grew steadily at colleges and universities from coast-to-coast. In 1921, it took on a new name, the *League for Industrial Democracy (the League),* and expanded its scope to addressing society at large.

Later, the fruits of the League would produce the *New Left,* a ubiquitous narcissistic community of activists, educators, agitators and others in the 1960's and 1970's who sought to implement a broad range of reforms, in stark contrast to the earlier more limiting Marxist movements that focused mainly on labor unionization and addressing social class issues. In America, the New Left was associated with the *hippie movement* and *college campus protest movements.* Anyone who wished to advance a progressive idea would simply introduce it into one of the local chapters on campus, and within weeks, sometimes even days, the idea would be firmly embedded into progressive thought. This process was fully exploited by intellectual elitists from every sphere of society.

As college students across the generations were cleverly taught various forms of progressivism ranging from Marxism, to socialism, to the precursor ideologies of postmodernism, many would go on to become *teachers* at all levels of American education.

Since the 1990's, many Boomer-educators, lacking a fully developed sovereign framework, have eagerly signed up to advance progressivism. The website, *EdChange.org,* is one of the narcissistic communities at the forefront of this powerful and dangerous movement. An excerpt from their mission statement tells the story:

"We recognize that teachers want and need strategies for implementation -- practical ideas, curricular tools, classroom activities, and pedagogical approaches that support diversity and equity. We know that the students ... today can't afford to wait for us to solve the bigger issues in education. So we work to balance the practical with the philosophical, providing immediate strategies while helping educators consider needs for long-term, institutional change."

The *Association of American Colleges and Universities* agrees:

"We must all become liberal educators who hold our students and ourselves accountable for the desired outcomes of a liberal education."

Do you think that, somehow, children in elementary school are immune to this progressive push by educators? Read this from an online introduction to a syllabus at the website of *Engines4Ed.org:*

"For Progressive reforms to succeed on a widespread basis, we need to break the lockstep of the classroom ... The goal here is to take the natural interests of each student and use them as a vehicle for *teaching what we want students to learn **(my emphasis). If a student likes trucks, why not teach him to read about trucks, do the math that is needed to understand fuel economies and know the economics and politics needed to run a trucking company?"***

In present-day, 64% to 71% of American educators label themselves, politically, as liberal or progressive. With the advent of social networking and instant messaging, they now have all the necessary tools to organize and mount an attack of unprecedented magnitude on our nation's children, many of whom lack a fully developed framework to deconstruct or filter the politically charged agenda that is being packaged and presented as "the very latest trends" in education that enable our children to "stay competitive" in an ever more global workplace.

We have now identified two major spheres of American culture that have elevated narcissism into a rapidly accelerating pandemic: the capitalist partnership between the media and corporate America, and the intellectual elitist post-modernist machine in academia. They are two reasonably exclusive paradigms which can't seem to get along, but which also have tended to leave each other alone.

The big losers here are the children in *Generation Y* (or, the *millennial generation*) and their younger siblings. Unless a groundswell of intervention occurs to help them snap out of their multi-anchored narcissistic stupor, this pivotal generation may be the last chance America has to protect itself and return to the freedoms our founders fought with their lives to procure.

Even if we begin a bold and brave intervention, we still have one more powerful force to subdue; in *Chapter Five*, we'll attempt to navigate the slippery slope of *technology*.

Sovereign Framework

Chapter 5

Heads or Tails

Now that we have established the existence of the pandemic in *Chapter Four,* we must now also examine how *technology* has become a major delivery system that narcissism uses to grow and maintain its presence. Then, we can formulate a strategy for attacking the contagion head on and destroying it.

As we come to fully understand how technology easily accelerates the spread of cultural pathological narcissism, we must put on both our *philosophy-geek* and *statistics-geek* hats.

At first glance, it might seem reasonable to posit technology as non-ethical and amoral in and of itself. However, a closer look reveals something quite different. In the only primary definition that does not recursively utilize the word's original components, *Dictionary.com*, citing several sources, defines **technology** as:

"The sum of the ways in which social groups provide themselves with the material objects of their civilization."

Technology, then, must first be an expression and extension of its creator's intent, or in the case of a group, its collective intent. Additionally, note how the definition does not limit the technology's use to *only* the entity that creates it. Others may have varying degrees of access to it, and they often find additional utility and functionality in it. Therefore, it is a *deterministic causal agency* that is *not* non-ethical and amoral. To be even more scientifically precise, it is a deterministic causal agency with an *infinite mean*. In other words, absent any factors that would govern its utilization, it is impossible to calculate and predict a precise set of *distribution outcomes* resulting

Heads or Tails

from its use. This is very nearly an exact description of *chaos theory*.

To express this as simply as possible, let's examine the example of someone flipping a coin X number of times. Your job is to guess the odds of a certain outcome, *heads* or *tails,* on the next flip. Aside from being a fun and interesting way to pass the time, this task becomes increasingly more difficult with each flip. Imagine flipping coins forever and trying to guess what the odds of heads or tails will be on the next flip; it is impossible to find an *average* or *mean,* because, mathematically, this problem has no mean (or, formally, it has an infinite mean). Why? Let's say after 20 flips you have a running count of 9 for heads and 11 for tails. The odds are nearly 50/50. But once in a while, you get several heads in a row. So, you might want to guess tails on the next flip, thinking that tails is overdue for an increment. But you might be wrong, because on each single flip, the odds *are* 50/50 for either heads or tails. In other words, the chances are just as good that heads will prevail again. This is a classic example of *binomial probability.*

Now, with binomial probability in mind, consider each use, by a single user of a single technology, to be one flip of a two-sided coin. However, in this case, we do not have heads or tails, but *positive* and *negative* effects (of this single use of the technology) on the user. There is an additional factor as well: we approach this flip not randomly but *deterministically* in that the user employs the technology slightly differently each time due to a confluence of external and internal factors such as climate, employment status, orders dictated by a community, mood, physical health, attitude towards the technology resulting from its previous use, etc. It is easy to see how it is impossible to predict the precise long-term *vector* that represents the final outcome of that user's utilization of the technology.

When this uncertainty is then multiplied by billions of users, the product is, most often, chaotic.

History is profligate with instances of how a technology, presumably invented for the greater good, is adopted and abused by narcissists who possess little or no sovereign framework. The outcome usually leads to social, economic, and sometimes even physical harm; a phenomenon I call *unintentional causality*.

Since around 1990, new technology has often reminded me of the new toy given to the narcissistic child. They play with it so hard and fast that it ends up broken in pieces, only to leave the child craving the next new toy. This happens because the child instantly develops grandiose and inappropriate expectations of the toy in hopes that its boundless, compulsive, and repeated use will somehow manifest a form of inner fulfillment and validation the child never experienced or received hitherto.

Two contemporary technology examples of this are the so-called *dot-com-bubble* and *mobile-texting*.

The popular hallmarks of the bull market in stocks from 1995-2000 were computers and the internet. The unbridled growth of their combined use gave way to the founding (and, in some cases, spectacular demise) of many new internet-based companies most commonly referred to as *dot-coms*. Companies were seeing their stock price shoot up like a rocket simply because they had a presence on the world-wide-web. A combination of rapidly increasing stock prices, market confidence that the companies would eventually turn future profits, individual speculation in stocks, and widely available venture capital, created an environment in which many narcissistic investors willingly overlooked traditional quantitative *valuation methods*. Instead, they opted to rely on the qualitative fundamental hope offered by this new technology, creating a huge narcissistic anchor for them in the process. Not surprisingly, the dot-com bubble, as measured by the *NASDAQ Composite* stock index, peaked at 5,132.52, and over the course of nearly three years, collapsed to a low of 1114.11, wiping out $5 trillion dollars of market value for investors.

In the case of texting, a handful of programmers in the late 1990's began developing the system that sends text messages over a mobile platform. They used their growing storehouse of development information to construct the basic texting application many of us now use today. Did they stop to think that kids of the *millennial generation,* many of whom lack a fully developed sovereign framework, would become anchored to the technology to the point where they are sitting side by side on a bus and texting each other instead of talking? As the programmers applied their reasonable, even honorable intent to the development of this technology, did they ever imagine that kids who are habitually texting away while hunched over their mobile devices would begin to suffer health problems related to bad posture and poor vertebral circulation? I have it on good authority that they did not.

Unintentional causality is not the exclusive franchise of capitalism. As we examined in *Chapter Four*, the historical search for solutions to this very problem itself has led to the creation of socio-economic ideologies, whole cultures, and even nations, many of which have also been thus abused in most cases by narcissists and narcissistic anchor-communities. A most profound example of this is the *collapse of both the Soviet Union and the Iron Curtain.*

If narcissism is left unchecked, it spreads into all spheres of a culture, and moves over into different kinds of cultures because it is *non-political, non-monistic,* and *classless.* To accomplish this, it utilizes all available modes of technology, along with the nascent pseudo-science of *memetics*.

The sociological concept of memetics is so new, a consistent definition has not yet made its way into mainstream dictionaries. **Wikipedia,** the free online encyclopedia, describes **memetics** as

"... an approach to evolutionary models of cultural information transfer ... (the study of that which) is copied from one person to another person, whether habits, skills, songs, stories, or any other kind of information."

A good instance of how narcissism employs the media and memetics to spread itself is what I call the *narcissistic brogue.* Again, just as I addressed the *Rolling Stop* in *Chapter One,* I will draw on a fairly large pool of empirical evidence.

The year was 1994, and my wife Mary & I had been living in Southern California for about a year. The whole CA scene was still new to me, and I was in wonder of its vast cultural differences as compared to my home state of Minnesota. One of the more pronounced differences (pun intended, as you will see!), was the distinct dialect or brogue of Los Angeles. It may be an over-simplification, but it is sufficient to support my point: the LA brogue is typified by what has come to be known as *valley-girl-speak*. A few examples are

- **"Oh my God!"** *-pronounced-* **AY-OH MAY GAWD**
- **"Tacos are not my favorite food."** -pronounced- **TAW-KAY-OHS OH-ARR NAWT MAY FAVRIT FEUD**
- **"Me too"** *-pronounced-* **ME TEE-OO**
- **"Mom, I need some money."** -pronounced- **MAWM AY NEED SIM MINNY**

Starting around 1996, America was in the midst of a bull market in equities and Americans were getting richer, at least on paper. This new wealth was burning a hole in people's pockets and the *empowerment paradigm* was demanding more money than ever from household budgets. One place where consumers were most willing to plunk down the change was the *cable television industry*. From 1989 to 1998, the number of on-air cable TV networks more than doubled from 79 to 171.

By 1999, when we moved back to Minnesota, I noticed a distinct change in the dialect of young Minnesotans. Gone was the subtle (or not!) Scandinavian brogue characterized by actress **Frances McDormand** in the Cohen brothers' 1996 film, **Fargo.** I was beginning to detect, in its place, the nasal twang of LA-valley-speak. It only took a few weeks to conclude that this shift must have begun while I had been living in LA. Throughout the 1990's, Minnesota youngsters were plopped in front of the ever-reliable surrogate baby-sitter, the TV, left to watch Hollywood-made content featuring Hollywood actors sporting the LA dialect. **Once again, wow!** But, at the time, I dismissed this trend as trivial. Little did I realize that the cultural shift signified by the infiltration of that brogue into the heartland of America was just the tip of the narcissistic iceberg that would creep into every home and school with increasing velocity as the nation moved into the 21st century.

Heads or Tails

Cultural information transfer, indeed!

WARNING: Take off all geek hats. Then, put on your *math-geek* hat, and **do not** allow your eyes to glaze over!

The formula for measuring the efficiency of how memetics accelerates the spread of narcissism in a given host is embodied in the following equation, where **S** is the development level of the host's *sovereign framework* (measured in a range from 0 to 100) and **ME** is the *memetic efficiency* (also measured from 0 to 100):

ME = |S - 100|
see footnote[4]

The higher the **ME** is, the more easily narcissism can utilize memetics as a means of propagating in the host. By the way, it is pure *coincidence* that the acronym for memetic efficiency is also the word *me*.

---

[4] The reference of a function between two PIPE symbols, | |, indicates an ***absolute value,*** that is, a positive number. So, |-.42| will result in a value of .42

Similarly, a *construct* for measuring the efficiency of a technology's ability to effect a host can be calculated in the following formula where **N** is the *total number of instances* of the host's use of the technology, **ME** is the *memetic efficiency* calculated from each use, and **TE** is the *technology-efficiency* metric:

$$TE = (ME_1 + ME_2 .. + ME_N)/N$$

In both algorithms, note that **S** is implicitly the most important variable because it may change over time depending on the host's ability to develop, strengthen, maintain, and defend their sovereign framework. This factor is the only one that enables the individual to protect themselves from narcissism, and neutralize or at least mitigate the random chaos brought about by unintentional causality. The higher the S factor, the greater the chance the individual will achieve a balanced life resulting in the fulfillment of both self and society in equal measure.

You may now release yourself from the rigorous attention required by our various trips into geek-land.

We will revisit these formulas in a philosophical scope in *Chapter Seven.*

In this chapter, we have discovered formulas we can use to rid ourselves of narcissism by developing and maintaining a **high "S" factor.** However, this process may take some time, particularly if we have only begun to develop a robust sovereign framework. Be very mindful that *many adversaries* do not want narcissism's reign to end, for it will signal the destruction of their temporarily pleasurable and satisfying narcissistic anchors.

In *Chapter Six,* as we begin to build and deploy a viable model for the eradication of narcissism in all spheres of society, we will learn that the selfish causes of these adversaries must be vanquished if we are to be completely successful.

Sovereign Framework

Chapter 6

Just who IS the enemy?

In *Chapter Four,* we examined how, ironically, the collective oligarchic alliance of greedy corporate America, the various media outlets, and the banking industry (henceforth, *big-business*) and the intellectual elitist postmodernist machine in American education (henceforth, *academia*) have worked fairly independently of each other and for different reasons to exploit the decline of family values for the advancement of their own narcissistic agendas. This inadvertent collaboration has helped greatly to cause the pandemic of narcissism in America today.

Then, in *Chapter Five,* we also looked at how narcissism has easily used *memetics* and *technology* to spread itself like wildfire across all spheres of American culture. But, there exists the potential for an even more efficient and powerful conveyance mechanism that threatens the very liberties our American founders fought so hard, some with their very lives, to procure. This mechanism is the combination of the spheres of *Economy* and *Policy* in America.

With the *Economy* factor, especially since the 1950's, the gradually accelerating destruction and mayhem foisted on the American family's pocketbook is nothing short of shocking. Back in the mid-20th century, the majority of American businesses manufactured high-quality products that often lasted well over ten years and sometimes even twenty. But, no thanks to a loosely structured alliance between banking, corporate, and marketing/promotion interests, the notion of American-made, quality, long-lasting products has been slowly and methodically replaced with business models characterized by lightning-fast product pipeline cycles, *planned obsolescence* (henceforth, PO), and the *funded proposal* (henceforth, FP), less formally referred to as the "give-away-the-razor and sell-the-blades-dear" approach. The resulting chaos makes the American consumer a slave to big-business, credit-card companies, and yes, ultimately, even certain parts of government.

In the case of PO, this systematic bleeding of the American consumer is highly deterministic and has roots in America's Great Depression. In 1932, industrialist-philosopher Bernard London wrote a pamphlet entitled *Ending the Depression through Planned Obsolescence*. In much the same way Karl Marx's theories took several decades to get noticed, London's ideas did not enter the mainstream consciousness of the U.S. manufacturing industry until 1954, when American industrial designer Brooks Stevens used PO as the theme and title for a keynote address to a convention of industrialists in Minneapolis. Citing PO's benefits of

"...instilling in the buyer the desire to own something a little newer, a little better, a little sooner than is necessary,"

Stevens was able to make an entire career out of consulting with companies, showing them how to "grow" their businesses more rapidly by methodically engineering a shorter life-span into their products, thus forcing the consumer into making a replacement purchase sooner than they expected. An excellent present-day case study of PO involves Apple Inc's iPod's that have "click-wheel" technology. Thousands of disgruntled consumers found their devices failing after just eighteen months; the precise duration of the gadget's warranty. Another example, also from Apple, is their iPhone product, which was released in June 2007. Less than three years later, Apple announced it would no longer support the device, angering millions of customers.

If PO isn't enough to burn your bagel, then try FP on for size. Originally popularized by Harvard Business School professors in the late 1970's and early 80's, this business model seeks to hook customers by selling an expensive feature-laden device at or near a company's cost (or, in the case of mobile phone carriers, at a substantial loss). Why would a business do this? Because there was bigger money on the back-end of the transaction: the device's design incorporates one or more so-called consumable products that become depleted over time and must be replaced repeatedly while the customer continues to use the device. Perfect present-day examples of this are mobile phone batteries, laser-printer ink cartridges, and automobiles. Another twist on the FP, is selling a basic service as cheaply as possible, and then bundling it with other services that, after a certain window of time, are suddenly far more expensive to keep. What's the idea behind it? To get customers to try the services just long enough to get addicted so they keep paying the higher rate after the introductory period has expired.

All this begs a question or two. Is all this corporate trickery necessary? Can't companies simply make a great, high-quality, long-lasting product, sell it at a fair profit, and leave it at that? To be fair, many do. But many other corporate executives, board members, and high-level managers are sufficiently narcissistic, greedy, and controlling that they cannot resist the temptation to fleece the American public of their hard-earned money. Some might argue that I am over-simplifying the issue. Fine. Corporate America is not totally comprised of greedy narcissists. But those who are not would certainly like to keep their jobs and they probably figure they stand a better chance at keep their jobs if the company is growing and making a profit. What better way to accelerate growth than to speed up the product cycle? The answer is that, thanks to the pandemic of narcissism, a growing number of Americans don't have the backbone to push back and say *No* to an unnecessarily sped-up product-cycle. Why? Because the conspiratorial squad of ad agencies and the various media outlets convince weak-willed Americans, most of whom lack a fully developed sovereign framework, that they are just not trendy or stylish enough to be full-fledged members of the empowerment paradigm (which was introduced in *Chapter Two*) unless they procure the latest version of a product, usually on credit, or with money that should otherwise go toward a far wiser purchase, or better yet, into a savings account.

In case you haven't connected the dots here, the empowerment paradigm is the *keeping up with the Jones's syndrome* on steroids, and whole companies have been created or re-configured to profit from it. I believe AT&T Inc., Google Inc., and Apple Inc. are chief among them.

Just who IS the enemy?

So far, we have only examined the big-business side of this economic phenomenon. The sphere of *academia* fits equally into the picture, because they are the beneficiaries of a socially engineered system which all but mandates that every child attend a school of "higher learning" so they can earn one or more degrees, get a great job, and become fully functioning participants in the empowerment paradigm. Of course, the child's parents often pay exorbitant tuition in the process. When parents are unable, the student must often take out a loan to pay for their education. In the past fifteen years, tuition costs, as a percentage of household income, have increasingly become the fastest growing expense for families, far outpacing even the outrageous health care costs for a typical family. It is yet another example of economic servitude in America. And to boot, the spendy tuition includes a near brainwashing of the child for the sake of advancing academia's narcissistic post-modernist agenda.

On the *Policy* front, it now becomes very easy to see how both big-business and elitist academia benefit greatly from controlling congress, and often even the White House. Every industry has one or more huge lobby groups to buddy up to policymakers and inveigle them to pass laws that enable industry to make more money. This is precisely how we have come to the brink of being a so-called nanny-state where we have hundreds of laws to "protect us" from our "irresponsible" selves: the child-car-seat laws for each state, supposedly in place to protect young ones from injury, also does a good job of making sure the manufacturers make more dough because families must now keep buying seats until a child is a certain weight, age, or height. Many states are now mandating that municipal building codes be updated to require homes and offices to install not only smoke detectors but carbon monoxide detectors as well. Ring up more sales for the manufacturers of those devices. The truth is, in the past ten years, an average of just 457 people per year have died from carbon monoxide poisoning. If we assume an average U.S. population of 285 million for the same period, that translates to less than 1/1000 of 1 percent.

There are almost countless examples of how, regardless of affiliation, narcissistic policymakers collaborate with narcissistic lobbyists paid by narcissistic big-business to

Just who IS the enemy?

make Americans do things that would simply have been unthinkable sixty years ago. Much of the policy is to "protect" us from substandard products or lackluster services big-business very nearly forced us to buy in the first place, no thanks to their PO.

Depending on how much or little of a robust sovereign framework you possess, YOU are a slave to and controlled by this greedy economic and policy mechanism to varying degrees.

I'm personally not into blaming anyone for anything. But, if you are a viewer or reader of the media these days, you know how a so-called "news report" is usually very quick to try and assign blame. So, who or what is to blame for this long-term treacherous trend in the American economy? Is it big-business, or academia? Can we blame it on narcissism? No. If blame must be assigned to anyone, it is me and you. I hold myself responsible, and you should too. Look in the mirror, and you will see the enemy. You and I have allowed ourselves to mistakenly believe the narcissistic myth passed down to us by each successive generation since American soldiers' triumphant return from WWII: Americans have victory, success, prosperity and empowerment in their genes; we can do no wrong! When you combine this dangerous attitude with the steady and inexorable erosion of traditional American family values of personal character, moral integrity, honesty, psychological & ethical boundaries, personal security, and concern and responsibility for the common good (hallmarks of a strong and robust individual sovereign framework), the result is that the rich get insanely richer, the poor get hooked on more government entitlements which cause unsustainable budget deficits, and you and I in the middle class get stuck with the tab in the form of increasingly higher taxes and higher prices for substandard goods and services we buy more frequently than we should; a third example of out-of-control servitude in America.

If you are still having difficulty seeing how you could possibly be complicit in this process, then I pose two simple questions: Are you saving for retirement, or, do you have any investments? Most will answer in the affirmative. What sort of return are you expecting from those investments? If your answer is anything higher than about 8%

per year, then you are a far bigger part of the problem than you realize.

It matters very little what actual financial instruments you are invested in. The average annual return on common stocks, since their use was revived in the seventeenth century, is approximately 8 percent. However, since the inception of the *Institutional Brokers' Estimate System (I/B/E/S)* in 1976, there has been a dangerous and increasingly relentless upward pressure of expectation on all stock prices, particularly U.S. prices.

The I/B/E/S started out harmlessly enough; it provided a system for stock analysts to collect fundamental earnings data on a company and compare it to data for the same company collected by other analysts. A consensus earnings estimate could then be calculated across a time-series, and company growth, as mapped in the time series, was often matched by the real-time performance of the company's share price.

However, even as early as 1985, Fortune 500 companies, many of which had narcissistic C-level executives and managers at the helm, began to see a positive cause/effect relationship between their ongoing communications with stock analysts and a better-than-average appreciation of company share price. This phenomenon spread to more and more companies throughout the 1990's, including the historic bull market in stocks from 1995-2000 when average stock market returns were closer to a range of 20-30%, depending on which stock index is looked at. Granted, the prolific growth of computing offered legitimate and permanent cost savings in the form of productivity improvements for firms, but the coefficient created by the consensus estimates of analysts also played a major part of that bull market run.

To put it simply, companies, fully aware that they were being analyzed for future growth prospects, began to look for creative and exotic ways to grow their earnings, and thus share price. This gave way in the early 2000's decade to rampant corporate malfeasance, fraudulent operations, and the indictment of dozens of high-profile U.S. executives. Many other companies kept their operations legal, but executives still looked for ways to log above-average returns for their shareholders, you and I, who were expecting the bull-market gravy train to sustain itself for years and years.

One of the worst developments in the history of American finance occurred in November 1999 with the passage of the Gramm–Leach–Bliley Act, a rollback of the Glass-Steagall Act of 1933 which prohibited bank holding companies from owning other financial companies. This opened the door for virtually all U.S. companies to get into the banking business. Suddenly, companies whose core business had nothing to do with banking were opening banking-related operations - all in an effort to keep you and me, their investors, happy with above-average returns on their share price. Company managers, many lacking the wisdom afforded by a sovereign framework, began authorizing massive trading in the so-called no-Doc/lo-Doc subprime mortgage market (CDO's, or Collateralized Debt Obligations). When the physical inventory of this paper got all bought up, these companies, no longer constrained by federal laws, began to trade *unregulated synthetic derivative equivalents* of the bundled CDO's, often placing much or all of the entire capital structure of the company at risk in a high-stakes game they had little or no experience with. They did this all in an attempt to sustain the incredibly high returns that WE as their investors had come to expect.

Naturally, the party came to an abrupt halt in the fall of 2008. What was the face amount of all the synthetic derivatives traded up to that point in time? An insane $432 trillion! That is magnitudes more than all the physical money that exists on the face of the earth.

The U.S. is now in the midst of an extended economic hangover that could easily last until 2020 and bring about another round of inflation as the U.S. Government tries to finance the trillion-plus dollar deficit the financial crisis created - all because you and I trusted a bunch of narcissistic CEO's to somehow get us a better-than-average return, because, after all, we are Americans, and "Dammit, we can do anything!"

While the hangover continues, you and I have some serious soul-searching to do. As we tighten our belts and learn to embrace the ugly economic salad-bowl-haircut we are sporting, I am convinced we will also find the antidote for the pandemic of narcissism. But don't be fooled.

Just who IS the enemy?

It is going to take an awful lot of very hard work. In *Chapter Seven,* assuming you agree that we both need to begin reversing the influence of narcissism in our lives, we will discover ways to readjust and reprogram our thinking so that you and I and all America will be able to return to its founding values of a strong family and a strong sense of ethics and commitment to community. This will enable us to embark on a moderate but far more hopeful path than the one we've been on since the end of WWII. Again, or maybe for the first time for some, we will be able to look in the mirror not with a sense of shame and fear, but with humility and hope for the future.

Sovereign Framework

Chapter 7

Settling the Score

If you are reading this chapter, I must assume you agree with me that you and I are equally at fault for the pandemic of narcissism that has plagued America for decades. Of course, that doesn't mean you are automatically a narcissist. But both of us need to be sure. Before we continue, you need to take Dr. Drew Pinsky's **Online Narcissism Test** at:
http://www.fireside-room.com/test
and see for yourself. Do it now. I will wait for you.

If you scored 10 or less, you are definitely NOT a narcissist, and you already have a robust sovereign framework. However, you may be interested to read on and see how I encourage those with varying degrees of narcissistic tendencies to rid themselves of it once and for all.

If you scored between 11 and 15, you display narcissistic tendencies on rare occasions, but are basically free of the problem. You too have a fairly strong framework. Read on anyway, it certainly won't hurt you.

Now, if you scored between 16 and 25, you display a fair amount of narcissistic traits and are a member of the largest growing segment of American population. Your sovereign framework is weak at best. I wrote this booklet for you. You are in the pool pretty deep, but not so deep as to make it impossible to reverse the course you have put yourself on.

If you racked up an astonishing 26 to 29 points, you likely are a chronic social pathological narcissist. Your framework is very nearly non-existent. It is going to be very difficult for you to take advice from me or anyone else on how to heal your problem, let alone actually go through the emotionally painful process. If you really want to do something about this, you may benefit from seeing a licensed psychologist.

Settling the Score

Finally, if you scored 30 or more points, a professional might diagnose you as having NPD: Narcissistic Personality Disorder, in my non-professional opinion. It will be next to impossible to moderate your condition. You possess NO sovereign framework. Nevertheless, if you have had it with the stress and frustration of living life in this grandiose way, if you are finished clawing and scratching your way through life and all its high drama, if you are sick and tired of trying to drag the world around with you like a ball and chain, maybe there is *some* hope for you. I strongly recommend you see a licensed psychologist.

By the way, I just took the test. I scored a 6. However, if this test had been available in 1983, I would have probably scored a 29. You see, at that time I was diagnosed as having borderline NPD. The next 4 years were some of the toughest years I ever lived. And yet, they were also some of the most liberating years of my life. I discovered the truth, and it set me free.

In the context of a robust sovereign framework, it is quite easy to convert your score to a rating scale of 0 to 100 to arrive at your sovereign framework rating (SFR). Simply take your score, divide it by 40, and multiply by 100 to arrive at value A. Then, subtract A from 100 and you have your SFR. The higher your rating is, the more robust your framework is. My score of 6 calculates to a SFR of 85. My past score of 29 calculates to an SFR of 27.5.

Once you have calculated your SFR, you can go back to *Chapter Five* and work with the formulas for calculating how susceptible you are to being manipulated by memetics and technology.

So fine, many of us are well on our way to neutralizing narcissism in our own lives, but how can we reverse its effects on American society?

As a *consumer*, you can do many things immediately to reverse the narcissistic trends:

   - **Get completely out of debt.** No ongoing credit card debt, no student loans, no home mortgages, no car loans. This is not easy. You must start small by paying off your littlest debt as soon as possible. Then, take the money you used to pay off that debt every month and move up the food chain to the next biggest debt, paying it off. Then add that money to your monthly payoff stash and move up the food chain pay off the next highest debt, and so forth. There is an excellent debt-reduction book entitled **Rapid Debt Reduction Strategies** by John Avanzini available at:

http://www.fireside-room.com/debtreduction

- *Once you are totally debt-free, open a savings account and save 10% of your take-home pay every month.* With this account, you are NOT saving up to buy gadgets, fashions, tech toys, or status symbols. Who needs those anyway? You have a strong sovereign framework and YOU define yourself by who you are INSIDE, not by any external factors. If your friends don't like it, maybe they're not the best kind of friends to be having anyway. This savings account is to be used for emergencies only - like when you or someone in your household becomes unemployed. Calculate your monthly expenses and keep depositing money into your savings account until you have 24 months of savings cushion built up. DON'T let it burn a hole in your pocket! Get a backbone and some discipline! This will go a long way toward preventing you from being a slave to the economic mechanism we discussed in *Chapter Six*.

- ***Don't automatically assume that the best path for your life is to attend college.*** While there are many important exceptions, most popular schools are pirates charging exorbitant tuition while also brainwashing students with their highly polished post-modernist agendas. My empirical evidence suggests that just two years at a liberal arts college can easily erase from 15 to 30 points off of a student's SFR. Still, college may be exactly what you need. Be prepared to pay the steep costs, and then gird your loins and stand firm and strong through the brainwashing process. Read this book every six months or so while you are in school so you can identify the narcissistic elitist academics who care far more about advancing their pocketbooks and progressive agendas than about helping you advance your career. If you've already been to college, then start passing on this thinking to your kids and grandkids.

As a **business owner,** you have a world of opportunity ahead of you:
 - *It's a well-known fact that you are far more likely to succeed if you are the FIRST company to provide a certain product or service.* But, do it

THE RIGHT WAY. If you sell products, sell long-lasting, high-quality products with a solid warranty at a fair price that gives you a nice profit and delivers profound value to your customers. If you provide a service, don't cut corners here and there and nickel and dime your customers for every little thing. Be generous - always think VALUE ADDED. And regardless of what type of business model you have, ALWAYS GO THE EXTRA MILE.

- *Stick to your core business and do it well.* If you are a public company, institute a strict policy of not providing earnings, top-line guidance, or ANY product pipeline information to analysts or the marketplace in general. If you are getting pressured by venture capitalists and investment bankers to give guidance (because that's the way it's done in the big leagues, dammit!), then fire them! Work only with VC's and IB's who understand the immense benefits of what you are doing. Sure, your share price will not likely skyrocket like some do, but it will also not likely TANK when you miss a quarter or two due to the normal cycles of your business model.

- *If you find opportunities to extend your business into other spheres, DO NOT ADD THEM TO YOUR EXISTING BRAND!* This is where most line extensions fail miserably. Instead START A NEW BRAND from scratch.

- *Run your business debt-free.* Period. Have oodles of cash lying around for emergencies and opportunities.

- *DON'T simply start a business so you can build it up and sell out to the highest bidder.* Instead, start a business because you want to be *in* that industry for the long haul. Otherwise, you are merely raping your employees and customers so you can get rich.

- *DON'T GET GREEDY!* Don't give progressives any reasons at all to hate you and your capitalist business model. Dedicate at least five percent of your top-line sales to humanitarian and community efforts such as feeding the hungry or providing free daycare to single parents in your area. Do it behind the scenes. Don't publicly promote your charitable initiatives. Do them in secret. As an American citizen who understands, via your continually strengthening sovereign framework, that government is ill-equipped to provide essential services to the poor and underprivileged, you could provide jobs training and basic education support to the poor in your community. Provide transportation for workers under the poverty threshold. Get creative - but always do it in secret under a different name!

- ***Say NO to government contracts,*** no matter how much of a gravy train it seems to be.

- ***Say NO to unionization of your workers.*** In fact, treat your workers so well, that any efforts at unionization will be utterly laughable.

On the ***policy*** front, VOTE - VOTE - VOTE! Get your butt out and VOTE in every primary and election.

- ***Vote for people who advocate strict term limits*** in your state capitol and Washington. No exceptions!

- ***Vote for people who advocate that judges should uphold the U.S. and state Constitution,*** and that judges should be elected by ***the people*** and not appointed by policymakers or their judicial-board cronies.

- ***Vote for people who advocate lowering tax rates*** and who advocate a budget ***surplus*** - not a deficit.

- ***Vote for people who understand that power in the hands of MANY,*** is far more preferable than power in the hands of a few narcissists.

Finally, teach your kids and grandkids **all of the above.** Additionally, love them. Nurture them. Validate them. Give them boundaries. Say NO, a lot more then you say YES. Explain why. Teach them to protect themselves internally and externally, and then teach them to extend that analysis to all society; if a decision turns out to be good for them but not for society in general, then it's not the right thing to do. DO NOT teach them that they can do anything they want - instead, teach them to make ALL their life-decisions based not just on what is in it for them, but what is in it for their city, county, state, and country. Teach them that America is NOT some big power or money machine that can be easily manipulated so you get ahead while you force *de facto servitude* upon everyone else. Teach them to obey ALL the laws, even the traffic laws like stop signs and speed limit signs. Practice what you preach and teach. Be honest and teach them honesty. Have integrity and teach them integrity. Get a backbone and stand for something, then teach them the same. Stand up straight and passionately salute the American flag during the Star Spangled Banner and teach them to do the same. Teach them all the verses to our national anthem. Explain what they mean. Explain the immense sacrifices all war veterans have made so that we can live a moderate, peaceable life of freedom in the greatest non-narcissistic nation on earth.

You get the picture: we take back America by taking *ourselves* back to the simple and profound American values that made, and will again make, our country great.

Why? Because we've already experienced the alternative: crash and burn and wade through year after year of economic servitude, heartbreak and chaos. I don't know about you, but I for one am going to work *real hard* the rest of my life to get it right this time.

I've just handed you many of the tools necessary to build and strengthen *your own* sovereign framework, and thus live a narcissism-free life of *greatness* balanced by moderation, service, and humility.

Now, once again, I ask you to look in the mirror and ask yourself:

What are you going to do with it?

Made in the USA
Charleston, SC
14 October 2014